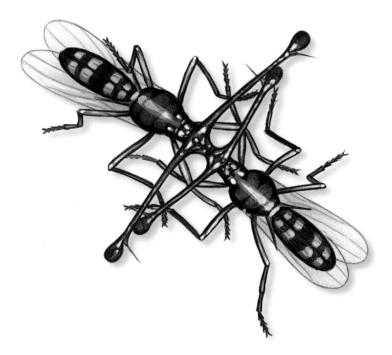

Published in 2015 by The Rosen Publishing Group, Inc.
29 East 21st Street, New York, NY 10010

Photo Credits: **KEY** tr=top right; cl=center left; c=center; bc=bottom center; br=bottom right; bg=background

iS = istockphoto.com; SH = Shutterstock; TPL = photolibrary.com

8–9bg iS; **13**tr SH; **23**bc, br TPL; **28–29**bg iS; **30**c iS; bg SH; br, c, cl, tr TPL

All illustrations copyright Weldon Owen Pty Ltd

WELDON OWEN PTY LTD
Managing Director: Kay Scarlett
Creative Director: Sue Burk
Publisher: Helen Bateman
Senior Vice President, International Sales: Stuart Laurence
Vice President Sales North America: Ellen Towell
Administration Manager, International Sales: Kristine Ravn

Library of Congress Cataloging-in-Publication Data

McFadzean, Lesley, author.
 Insects / by Lesley McFadzean.
    pages cm. — (Discovery education. Animals)
 Includes index.
 ISBN 978-1-4777-6952-2 (library binding) — ISBN 978-1-4777-6953-9 (pbk.) —
ISBN 978-1-4777-6954-6 (6-pack)
 1. Insects—Juvenile literature. I. Title.
 QL467.2.M3694 2015
 595.7—dc23
                          2013047457

Manufactured in the United States of America

CPSIA Compliance Information: Batch #WS14PK3: For Further Information contact Rosen Publishing, New York, New York at 1-800-237-9932

Discovery
EDUCATION

ANIMALS

INSECTS

LESLEY MCFADZEAN

PowerKiDS
press
New York

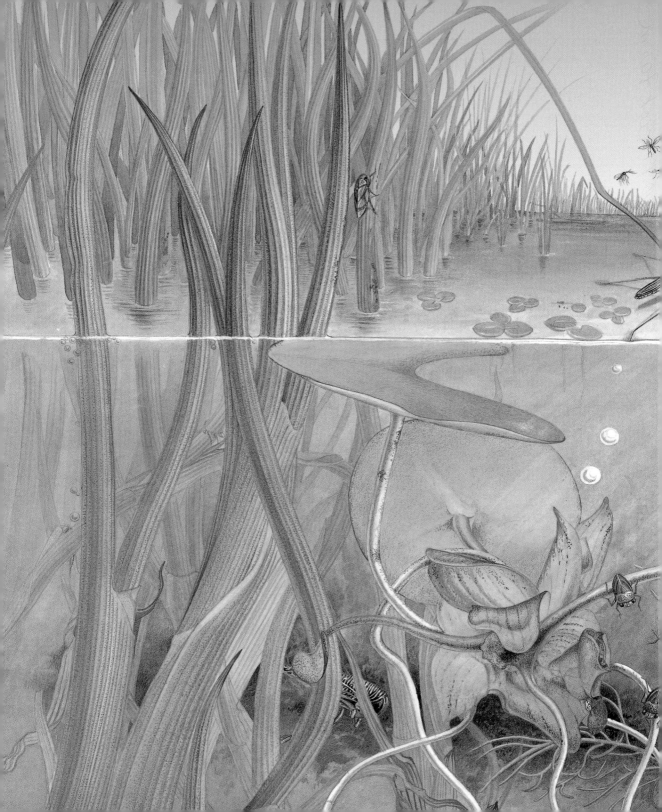

Contents

What Is an Insect?

Insects have exoskeletons. That is, their skeletons are on the outside of their body, not inside, like ours. An insect's body is divided into three sections—the head, the thorax (chest), and the abdomen (stomach). The head has the eyes, mouthparts, brain, and two antennae. The wings and three pairs of legs are attached to the thorax. The abdomen contains the internal organs.

Butterfly

Fungi (4.9%)

Bacteria (0.3%)

Algae (1.9%)

Other animals (19.9%)

Plants (17.6%)

Insects (53.2%)

Microscopic animals (2.2%)

Hoverfly

Most successful animals
More than half of all the living things on Earth are insects. Scientists have identified and named more than a million insect species, but there are millions of other unnamed insect species still out there.

ARE THEY INSECTS?

Spiders, scorpions, millipedes, and centipedes all have an exoskeleton, like insects. But they have more than six legs and do not have three body sections. They are not insects.

Scorpion

Spider

Mosquito

Beetle

Grasshopper

Dragonfly

Ladybug

First flyers

Insects were the first living things on Earth to fly. Most insects have wings, such as the ones shown here. Wings allow them not only to escape from nonflying predators, but also to fly around in search of food.

Cicada

Did You Know?

Insects have been found in almost all of the world's habitats. No insects have yet been found in the oceans.

Beetles

One in every four animal species in the world is a beetle. Beetles belong to the order Coleoptera, which means "sheath wing." They have two pairs of wings. The outer pair are hard wing cases, called elytra. They fold over the inner flying wings like a protective sheath.

A diet of dung

Many beetles are scavengers that eat dead animals, dead plants, and other waste. The dung beetle eats the feces, or dung, of other animals and, by doing so, cleans up a huge amount of unwanted waste.

1 A ball of dung

The female dung beetle lays an egg inside a large dung ball. The male dung beetle rolls the dung ball, with the female on top, to a burrow that they have made.

Bee-eating beetle

African jewel beetle

South American longhorn beetle

BEETLE PARADE

Beetles come in many different sizes, shapes, and colors. The smaller the beetle, the smaller the cavity or hole it can squeeze into. Color may be used for camouflage, so it varies according to a beetle's habitat.

Rove beetle

5 A new generation
The adult beetle eats liquid dung until it finds a mate and builds a dung ball of its own. Now it can produce the next generation.

4 Adult emerges
Once it has turned into an adult, in a process called metamorphosis, the adult beetle eats and digs its way out of the dung ball. It is free to fly away.

2 Larva eating
Inside the dung ball, the soft-bodied larva hatches out of the egg. It immediately starts eating the dung around the area where it was born.

3 Pupal stage
When the larva has eaten enough dung and is fully grown, it develops into a hard-bodied pupa. Now it can change into an adult beetle.

A male dung beetle can roll a dung ball 1,000 times heavier than its body weight.

Flies

The many species of flies include common houseflies, mosquitoes, gnats, and fruit flies. Most flies have two front wings and two small knobs, or stalks, called halteres. The halteres vibrate in time with the wings and help the fly to keep its balance when in flight. Some flies have no wings and are flightless.

Fly foot
On the end of each leg, the common housefly has two claws and a sticky pad. This allows the fly to walk upside down across a ceiling.

A dragonfly is not a fly
Not all insects with "fly" in their names are true flies. The dragonfly belongs in a different order of insects because it has four wings, not two. Its back and front wings beat at different speeds and do not fold away.

The snow fly's habitat is too cold for wing muscles to work, so it has no wings. It walks or leaps instead.

DISEASE CARRIERS

Tsetse flies in Africa feed only on the blood of large mammals—including humans. They transmit the deadly disease trypanosomiasis, or sleeping sickness. In most fly species that bite, only the females bite. But both male and female tsetse flies are biters.

Before feeding

Saliva transmits disease.

Abdomen swollen with blood

Eye with 4,000 lenses.

Wings fold
against back.

Proboscis
extends and
retracts.

Legs have
many joints.

Front legs
taste food.

Liquid food
A fly sponges or
sucks up liquid food
using its proboscis.
First, it has to turn
solid food into a
liquid. It vomits
saliva over the food
to liquefy it and
make it mushy!

Common housefly
The common housefly eats only
liquids. Its mouthparts form a long
tube, called a proboscis. This extends
out from the head for the fly to eat,
then retracts, or returns, into the
head when the meal is over.

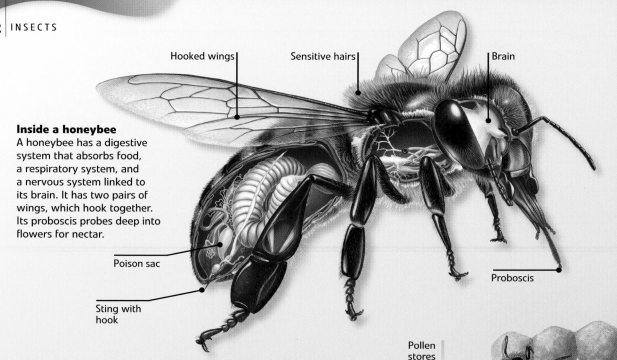

Hooked wings | Sensitive hairs | Brain

Inside a honeybee
A honeybee has a digestive system that absorbs food, a respiratory system, and a nervous system linked to its brain. It has two pairs of wings, which hook together. Its proboscis probes deep into flowers for nectar.

Poison sac

Proboscis

Sting with hook

Pollen stores

Drone bee

Empty cell

Bees and Wasps

B ees and wasps are hymenopterans, which means "membrane-winged." They are called this because they have two pairs of transparent wings. They are the main pollinators of all plants. Some bee and wasp species are solitary, but others live in a very structured "society" where each individual has its own tasks and its own high or low position.

Queen cell

Drone cell

In a honeybee hive
The queen honeybee lays all the eggs in the hive and lives for up to five years. Worker honeybees feed the queen and larvae, maintain the wax cells, and die in a few weeks. Male drones mate with the queen.

Open larva cell

HOW MANY STINGS?

A bee (left) can sting only once. Its hooked sting and some of its organs are left behind, so it dies. A wasp (right) can withdraw its smooth sting and fly off to sting again and again.

Digger wasps
The female digger wasp paralyzes insects with her sting, then places them with her eggs. The larvae hatch and eat the paralyzed insects alive.

Nectar stores

Honey stores

Queen bee

Worker bee

Butterflies and Moths

Butterflies and moths belong to the insect order Lepidoptera, which means "scale wing." Butterflies have millions of tiny, overlapping scales on the top of their four wings. In daylight, these scales show up as bright colors on butterflies and moths that are diurnal, or active during the day. Nocturnal moth species, which are active at night, are often brown or gray.

1 Eggs
The female butterfly lays her eggs on a leaf that will provide food for her larvae.

Change in form

Metamorphosis is a process where an insect changes its form, and many do this during their life cycle. A butterfly's life cycle has four stages: egg, larva, pupa, and adult butterfly.

2 Larva
A caterpillar hatches from an egg. It feeds constantly and molts as it grows bigger.

3 Pupa
The larva uses a gluey silk to build a cocoon, where the pupa can develop.

COCOONS

Cocoons can be soft or hard, transparent or thick, brightly colored or plain. It depends on the species. A larva will hide its cocoon under a leaf or in a crack, and will sometimes add twigs as a disguise.

Indian leaf butterfly

Paper kite butterfly

Cloudless sulfur butterfly

Some caterpillars weave their own hairs into their cocoon. These hairs feel itchy and stop predators from eating the cocoon.

4 Adult butterfly
A few weeks later, the adult butterfly breaks out of the cocoon.

5 A new cycle
The adult butterfly flies off to find a mate and the cycle begins again.

Moth, not butterfly
Moths usually have much fatter, furrier bodies than butterflies because many moths are nocturnal and need to keep warm on cool nights. Moths have feathery antennae, while butterfly antennae are very fine.

Bugs and Others

Bugs have a mouth that can pierce and suck. A favorite food of many is plant sap, which is why farmers and gardeners think they are pests. But some bugs prefer to eat other insects or animal blood. All bugs go through a simple or incomplete metamorphosis: from egg to nymph to adult. The nymphs, or immature bugs, of some bug species look like small, wingless adults.

Lace bug

A lace bug is small, with lacy wings. It can spend its entire life on one plant. It pierces the underside of the plant's leaves and sucks out the sap.

Praying mantis

The praying mantis eats insects, including other mantises. While it waits for prey such as a moth, it stays very still, with its forelegs held up as if it is praying.

Spittle bug

Spittle bugs get their name from the mass of foamy spittle that the nymphs form around themselves so they do not dry out.

Peanut-headed lantern fly

This bug head looks like a peanut and glows. It feeds on leaves that contain toxic chemicals. When in danger, it sprays these chemicals at its attacker.

Yellow treehopper

Treehoppers are small, leaping bugs that feed on the sap in branches and twigs. They have a plate like a shield, called a pronotum, over their back and head.

Horned treehopper

Treehoppers are sometimes called thorn bugs. The horns on this treehopper look like thorns and keep predators away.

Jester bug

This bug feeds on nectar from flowers. Its colorful red and black body keeps predators away because, in the animal world, bright colors usually mean a nasty taste.

Cotton stainer bug

Some cotton stainer bugs feed on cotton bolls. They pierce the plant and the sap stains the white cotton a bright yellow color, making it unusable.

Water Insects

About 97 percent of insect species are terrestrial, that is, they live on land. But three percent are aquatic and live at least part of their lives in freshwater. Some of these insects remain at the surface of the water, where they can breathe in oxygen, but others have adapted so they can spend time underwater.

Oxygen bubble
The diving beetle traps oxygen in a bubble under its hard wing cases. So when it dives, it has its own supply of oxygen.

BREATHING UNDERWATER

Insects must breathe oxygen to survive, but how do aquatic insects do this underwater? Human divers use air tanks or snorkels to get oxygen. Some insects use similar techniques so they can breathe underwater.

Breathing tube
The mosquito larva's breathing tube operates like a snorkel. Its body is underwater, but the breathing tube is above the water and provides the larva with oxygen from the air.

Tadpole

Water scorpion

Moving in water

The water strider walks—lightly—on the thin skin of the water surface. The heavier water boatman uses its strong legs to paddle around. The water scorpion anchors itself to water weed so it is not swept away.

Backswimmer
The backswimmer is a type of bug. It has a sharp, piercing proboscis. It swims underwater by doing the backstroke with its rear legs, searching for other water-dwelling insects to prey on.

Water strider

Water boatman

HONEYBEE LARVAE

The larvae are provided with a constant supply of food, not by their mother—the queen bee—but by worker bees. They stay inside a waterproof, waxy cell until they become adults.

| Hatched larva | Well-fed larva | Pupa | Adult ready to emerge |

Life Cycle

After laying their eggs, most insects do not care for or watch the eggs hatch. The eggs that survive hatch into larvae or nymphs. Larvae undergo complete metamorphosis, or a total change. Nymphs undergo simple metamorphosis, where the young insect looks similar to the adult.

Last molt
A leafhopper sheds the exoskeleton its body has outgrown.

Shedding skeletons

The problem with having an exoskeleton is that the hard external skeleton stops the soft body inside from growing. So when it grows too big for its exoskeleton, the insect sheds it. It does this several times in its life. The process is called molting.

Laying eggs

Insects lay their eggs near a food supply so the hatched young have all the food they need.

Cockroach eggs
This cockroach is laying up to 40 eggs. All are inside a single hard capsule.

Adult leafhopper
The full-grown adult leafhopper will not shed its exoskeleton again.

Honeybee eggs
Each honeybee egg has its own cell. Worker bees feed the larva with royal jelly.

Lacewing eggs
A lacewing deposits eggs on long stalks, up high and away from small predators.

Mosquito eggs
Mosquitoes lay their eggs in water. The egg clusters float like a tiny raft.

Ladybug eggs
A ladybug lays up to 15 tiny, yellow, jelly-bean-shaped eggs on a leaf.

Human louse

Cockchafer

Emperor moth

Butterfly

Mosquito

Long-horned beetle

Super Senses

Some insects hear through their antennae or body hairs, while some species have ears on their front legs or abdomen. Many insects have compound eyes, which are large eyes with hundreds—even thousands—of lenses. Insects use palpi, special hairs around their mouths or on their feet, to taste. Antennae are used not only to hear but also to smell and touch.

Multipurpose antennae
An insect's two antennae can detect the scent of either prey or a mate. A moth's antennae can also help it navigate in the dark; a mosquito's antennae can sense the heat or sweat of a human body.

Stalk-eyed flies
These flies have eyes on the end of long stalks. They have a much wider view than if their eyes were set on each side of their head. Males size each other up by comparing the length of their eye stalks.

Compound
eye

Ocelli

Antenna

Dragonfly sight

The dragonfly has two compound
eyes with 28,000 lenses each. It
also has three small eyes, called
ocelli, on top of its head. Because
it relies on its excellent sight, its
antennae are short.

WHAT COLOR LOOKS LIKE

Insects' eyes can see some but not all
colors. They do not see the yellow petals
of this flower. Instead, they see landing
areas and other details around a food
source, which is the center of the flower.

What a human sees

What an insect sees

Attack and Defense

Insects have different survival methods. Some attack on their own with built-in weapons, while others work together in large groups, as army ants do. In defense, insects have three choices. They can stand and fight. They can fly away or hide in a tiny crack where a larger predator cannot reach them. Or they can make themselves invisible by using camouflage.

BLENDING IN

Some insect camouflage is so good, it is almost impossible to see them. Because insects spend so much time living on plants, a disguise that makes them look like a part of a plant is the best.

Katydid

Orchid mantis

Stick insect

Real and fake

Some insects have stings, horns, spikes, poisons, sprays, or nasty smells that they use as weapons. Others have no way of fighting off predators. Instead, they use fake colors or pretend eyes to seem dangerous.

Hercules beetle

The male Hercules beetle has two very sharp, long horns. But it uses these horns mostly to fight other male Hercules beetles. The winner is allowed to mate with the females.

Bombardier beetle

In attack or defense, the bombardier beetle secretes chemicals into a special chamber, then squirts the hot, acid spray out of its abdomen. It has very good aim.

Silk moth

This moth's colors blend in with trees. If it does not fool a bird predator, the moth opens its wings to reveal large, owl-like eyes and scares the bird away.

Giant weta

The giant weta is the size of a small rat and one of the heaviest insect species. If its size does not keep predators away, it throws up its strong, spiny back legs.

?... You Decide

nsects pollinate plants, trees, and crops, and provide nutrients for them. They even eat insect pests. They are also a vital link in the food chain. However, insect bites and stings can injure and kill. Some insects spread bacteria, viruses, and parasites. So are the world's insects our friends or our foes? You decide.

FOOD CHAIN

Insects eat plants and, in turn, are eaten by larger animals up the food chain. The larger animals would starve without insects providing the vital link in the food chain.

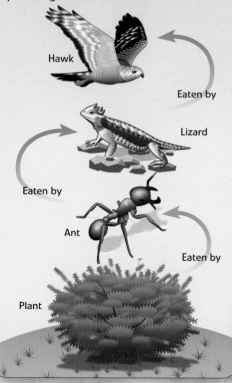

Hawk

Eaten by

Lizard

Eaten by

Ant

Eaten by

Plant

Pollinators
Many insects—not only bees, but also butterflies, moths, flies, and beetles—pollinate flowering plants by carrying pollen from the male to the female plant. Without these insects, many plants, including fruit trees, would become extinct.

Cleaners
Insects break down and recycle organic material such as dead wood, leaves, animal droppings, and dead animals. This provides nutrients for the soil and clears the ground so new plants can grow.

Locust swarm

The locust, a species of grasshopper, is normally solitary. But locusts can join together in a swarm of billions, then take to the air, find, and destroy an entire grain crop in a few hours.

MALARIA

Mosquitoes transmit malaria, which affects 247 million people each year and kills 1.5 million people. When a mosquito feeds on the blood of a person with malaria, it absorbs the parasite that causes the disease, then passes it on to the next person it "bites."

Health hazard?

Cockroaches are scavenging insects. However, only one percent of cockroach species are pests that invade homes. They move from rotting garbage to food and may transfer bacteria. Most cockroach species recycle organic remains outside the home.

Fact File

There are many different families of insects. They have some common features but many differences including size, shape, speed, lifespan, and the sounds they make.

Here are some interesting facts about insects:

 1 Fastest runner: Australian tiger beetle (*Cicindela hudsoni*)

2 Fastest flyer: corn earworm moth (*Helicoverpa zea*)

3 Largest: giant scarab (*Goliathus goliatus*, *G. regius* or *Megasoma elephas*)

4 Longest: stick insect (*Pharnacia serratipes*)

5 Largest butterfly or moth wingspan: white witch moth (*Thysania agrippina*)

6 Longest life cycle: wood-boring beetle (*Buprestis aurulenta*)

7 Loudest: African cicada (*Brevisana brevis*)

8 Most toxic venom: harvester ant (*Pogonomyrmex* species)

Corn earworm moth
(*Helicoverpa zea*)

Stick insect
(*Pharnacia serratipes*)

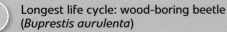

White witch moth
(*Thysania agrippina*)

African cicada
(*Brevisana brevis*)

Harvester ant
(*Pogonomyrmex* species)

Glossary

abdomen
(AB-duh-mun) The third, rear section of an insect's body that contains the internal organs.

antennae
(an-TEH-nee) Two "feelers" attached to an insect's head. The antennae are sense organs used for touch, taste, and smell.

camouflage
(KA-muh-flahj) Special features, color, and shape that an insect uses to hide in a habitat or to disguise itself.

cocoon (kuh-KOON)
A covering that an insect larva forms around itself and is then used to protect the pupa inside.

compound eye
(KOM-pownd EY) An eye that has many, often thousands of, lenses.

diurnal (dy-UR-nul) Describes an insect or other animal that is active during the day.

elytra (EE-ly-truh)
The hard front wings of beetles that fold over and protect the back, flying wings.

exoskeleton
(ek-soh-SKEH-leh-tun)
The hard outer skeleton that supports an insect's body. The exoskeleton is shed as the soft body grows inside it.

food chain
(FOOD CHAYN) A community of living plants and animals where each is eaten by another larger, living thing above it in the chain.

haltere (HAL-tir) One of two small knobs or stalks that is a modified back wing. The two halteres are used to stabilize the insect in flight.

larva (LAHR-vuh) The young form of an insect after it has hatched from an egg. The larva does not look like its adult parent.

metamorphosis
(meh-tuh-MOR-fuh-sus)
The complete change in shape and form that an insect larva must go through before it becomes an adult. A caterpillar larva changes into a butterfly or moth through metamorphosis.

molt (MOHLT) To shed an exoskeleton that is too small to allow the body underneath to grow bigger.

nymph (NIMF) The early developmental stage of an insect from a hatched egg. The nymph looks like a small, wingless form of the adult insect.

ocelli (oh-SEH-lee) Extra eyes with a simple lens that some insects have on the top or sides of their head.

palpi (PAL-pea)
Sense organs, like feelers or hairs, around an insect's mouth, used to taste and eat.

pollinate (PAH-luh-nayt)
To carry or transfer pollen from a male plant cell to a female cell.

proboscis (pruh-BAH-sus)
The hollow mouthparts of some insects that extend from the insect's head. The proboscis sucks up liquid food like a straw.

proleg (PROH-leg) One of four short, thick stumps in the abdomen of some insect larvae.

pronotum (PROH-notum)
The top surface at the front of the thorax in some insects that stretches across the back like a plate or saddle.

pupa (PYOO-puh)
The stage in insect metamorphosis between the larva and the adult insect. The pupa remains inside a cocoon before it emerges as an adult insect.

scavenger (SKA-ven-jur)
An insect that eats already-dead plants, animals, or animal waste.

thorax (THOR-aks)
The middle or chest section of an insect. Wings and legs are attached to the thorax.

Index

A
antennae 6, 15, 22, 23
ants 26, 28, 30

B
bees 12, 13, 20, 21, 28
beetles 7, 8, 9, 18, 22, 24, 26, 27, 28, 30
bombardier beetles 27
bugs 16, 17, 19
butterflies 6, 14, 15, 22, 28, 30

C
camouflage 8, 26
cicadas 7, 30
cockroachs 21, 29
cocoon 14, 15

D
disease 10, 29
dragonflies 7, 10, 23, 24
dung beetles 8, 9, 28

E
eggs 8, 12, 13, 14, 20, 21
elytra 8, 25
exoskeleton 6, 20, 21
eye 6, 11, 22, 23

F
flies 10, 11, 22, 24, 28

G
grasshoppers 7, 24, 29

H
haltere 10, 24
hoverflies 6

K
katydids 26

L
ladybugs 7, 21, 24, 25
larva 9, 12, 13, 14, 18, 20, 21, 24
locusts 29
looper caterpillars 24
louse 22

M
mantises 16, 26
metamorphosis 9, 14, 16
molt 14, 20
mosquitoes 6, 10, 18, 21, 22, 29
moths 14, 15, 22, 27, 28, 30

N
nymph 16, 17, 20

P
pests 16, 28, 29
proboscis 11, 12, 19
pupa 9, 14, 20

S
stalk-eyed flies 22
stick insects 26, 30
sting 12, 13, 26, 28

T
treehoppers 17
tsetse flies 10

W
wasps 12, 13
water insects 18, 19, 24
wings 6, 7, 8, 10, 11, 12, 14, 24, 25, 27, 30

Websites

Due to the changing nature of Internet links, PowerKids Press has developed an online list of websites related to the subject of this book. This site is updated regularly. Please use this link to access the list:
www.powerkidslinks.com/disc/inse/